SADIE'S SEED ADVENTURES

BY TINA DYBVIK • ILLUSTRATED BY ADAM RECORD

LEARNING ABOUT SEEDS

PICTURE WINDOW BOOKS
a capstone imprint

"Hi, Marv!" said Sadie. "What can we do today?"

"Hi, Sadie!" said Gardener Marv. "It's time to pull weeds and get the garden ready for next spring."

"This garden looks like a jungle," she said.

"Well, get ready, Sadie! Strange things can happen in the jungle!" he said.

"What are those stickers on Jonesy?" Sadie asked.

Gardener Marv pulled off a sticker and held it.

"Meet the cocklebur," he said.

"I've seen those burs in the country," said Sadie, "but not here in town."

"Then while you're working, see if you can find a cocklebur plant," said Marv. "Now remember: safety first. Anything can happen in this jungle."

"I found the stickers!" Sadie said.

"Well done," replied Marv. "They're the cocklebur fruit."

Sadie pulled a bur from the plant's tall stem. Marv cut it in half.

"The outer part of the seed is called a hull," explained Marv. "It's like a container, and it holds a tiny living plant. The plant will grow in the soil when the conditions are just right."

"But how did the seeds for these plants get into our garden?" asked Sadie.

Marv grinned. "Let's find out, Sadie," he said. "IT'S TIME TO PUT ON OUR ADVENTURE HATS!"

HULL

There are two types of fruits: dry and fleshy. Burs, nuts, and grains are all dry fruits. Berries are fleshy fruits.

Sadie put on the safari hat. She started to get dizzy.

"Why do I feel like I'm falling?" she asked. "And the cocklebur plants are growing!"

"We're shrinking," said Marv. "Here comes Jonesy. Jump on and take a ride."

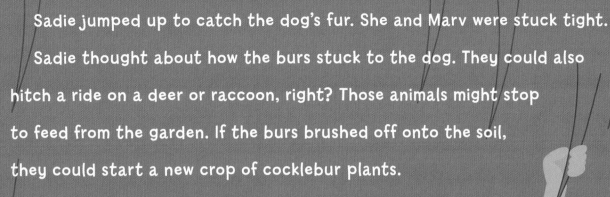

Sadie jumped up to catch the dog's fur. She and Marv were stuck tight.

Sadie thought about how the burs stuck to the dog. They could also hitch a ride on a deer or raccoon, right? Those animals might stop to feed from the garden. If the burs brushed off onto the soil, they could start a new crop of cocklebur plants.

That was it! Sadie knew how the cockleburs had found their way to the garden.

Some seeds are dispersed, or scattered, by animals. Cockleburs contain seeds. A bur has sharp barbs that get tangled in animal fur. Animals carry the bur and seeds to a new location. Other seeds are eaten by animals. The animals then leave the seeds in a new location when they poop.

Just then, Jonesy charged into a bunch of brown pods, and soft white fluff filled the air.

"More seeds?" asked Sadie.

"It's milkweed," said Marv. "That's how the seeds disperse. I meant to pull the milkweed plants before the pods burst. Now we might have milkweed everywhere!"

"I figured it out. The burs got here on animals," said Sadie.

"That is correct," Marv replied. "But what about the
milkweed seeds? Did they ride animals too?"

WOOF!
WOOF!

Sadie gazed at the fuzzy floating seeds. She
dropped her gloves and spread her arms wide.
"Let's go for another ride!" she said.

"Hold on to your hat!" warned Marv.

They floated over the garden. They finally
touched ground on the shore of the pond.

SWOOSH!

SWOOSH!

"So the wind disperses milkweed seeds?" asked Sadie.

"Correct again!" said Gardner Marv.

"But how do we get back to the garden?" she asked.

Wind is one way seeds disperse. Milkweed, dandelion, and maple seeds are all designed to catch air and float. They use wind to disperse.

Marv stepped onto a lily pad. "Take a look in the pond," he called.

Sadie teetered to the edge and peeked at the water. "What are those berries?" she asked.

"They are the fruit of the water lilies," said Marv. "Follow me!"

Some seeds depend on water for dispersal. The fruits of the water lily float for a while. Then they soak up water and sink to the bottom. The seeds inside them become new water lily plants.

Marv jumped on a berry and hugged it like a beach ball.

He was floating toward the creek that ran past their garden.

"Wait for me!" Sadie shouted.

They were almost to the garden when a huge gust of wind blew the hats off their heads.

"SEE THAT BRANCH?" yelled Marv. "GRAB ON!"

Sadie reached up and grabbed the branch. "OUCH!" she cried. A thorn had stuck her thumb.

"The berries look like blueberries," she said.

"These are buckthorn berries," Marv explained.

"You don't want to eat them. They'll make you sick."

Sadie jiggled the branch a little, and a few

berries fell to the ground.

WOOF!

Never eat or
taste unknown
plant fruits, even
if you see animals
eating them.

The shaking of the branch startled a finch out of the buckthorn bush.

A blue-black dropping fell from the bird and landed on Sadie's boot.

"Gross!" said Sadie. She leaned over to study the dropping.

A small green pit stuck out of the center.

"Is that a SEED?" she asked.

"Sure is," said Gardener Marv. "A buckthorn seed hull is hard.
It can wait for years before it starts to grow."

PLOP!

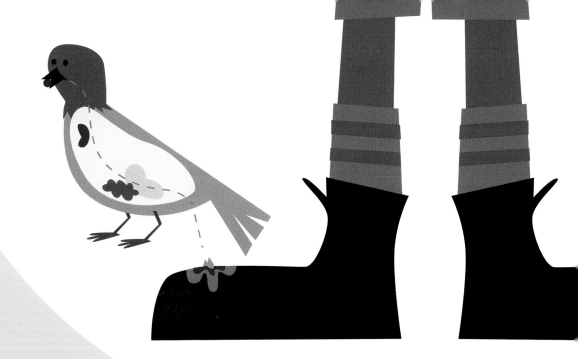

Sadie was more interested in where the seed had been. Passing through a bird's sharp beak and tiny dark insides was a dangerous way to plant new life!

"A buckthorn seed is strong," she decided.

"So strong, we don't plant it," agreed Gardener Marv. "That bush would take over the garden. It would be hard to control it."

> Some seeds have thick hulls. They have to be softened by passing though an animal. Once the animal poops, the seed may be soft enough to germinate in the soil.

Their adventure hats had washed ashore. Sadie looked at the garden plot. The jungle of weeds was gone. It was time for lunch.

"We've had some big adventures!" said Marv. "What did you think?"

"If I could be a seed," Sadie said. "I'd be a milkweed seed, so I could float on the wind."

Gardener Marv laughed. "And what did you learn?" he asked.

"Respect the jungle," she said, "because anything can happen!"

DISPERSAL METHODS OF SEEDS

cockleburs ⟶ hitch a ride

milkweed seeds ⟶ wind

water lily berries ⟶ water

buckthorn berries ⟶ animal poop

Sock Walk

Did you know that socks can collect seeds? Try out this fun experiment on your next nature walk. Plant the sock, and watch the seeds grow!

What you need:

- old sock
- shoebox
- garbage bag or plastic wrap
- potting soil
- scissors

What you do:

To collect your seeds:

1. Find an old sock that fits over your shoe.
2. Walk back and forth in a wooded or vacant lot that's full of weeds. The best time to collect seeds is in fall.
3. Take off the sock and look for seeds that are stuck to the sock.

To plant your sock:

4. Line a shoebox with a garbage bag or plastic wrap.
5. Fill the shoebox with potting soil.
6. Cut one side of the sock the long way.
7. Flatten the sock and plant it with the seed side up. Cover with soil.
8. Leave the box in a sunny spot. For the next few days, water the soil so it's moist but not too wet.

What you get:

In a week or so, the seeds should begin to grow. You never know what you may get!

GLOSSARY

buckthorn—a shrub or small tree with sharp thorns and clusters of small white flowers; commonly found in southern and central areas of the United States

cocklebur—a plant of the daisy family, with broad leaves and burred fruits

disperse—to scatter

hull—hard outside part of a seed

germinate—when a seed sends out a root and stem

milkweed—an American plant with milky sap

pod—a long case that holds the seeds of certain plants, such as milkweed or peas

seed—a part of a flower that will grow a new plant

soil—another word for dirt

stem—the part of a plant that connects the roots to the leaves

water lily—a plant that grows in water; it has large round floating leaves and large, cup-shaped, floating flowers

READ MORE

Dickmann, Nancy. *A Bean's Life.* Watch It Grow. Chicago: Heinemann Library, 2010.

Lundgren, Julie K. *Seeds, Bees, and Pollen.* My Science Library. Vero Beach, Fla.: Rourke Pub., 2012.

Sterling, Kristin. *Exploring Seeds.* Let's Look at Plants. Minneapolis: Lerner Publications, 2012.

Weakland, Mark. *Seeds Go, Seeds Grow.* Science Starts. Mankato, Minn.: Capstone Press, 2011.

INDEX

INTERNET SITES

FactHound offers a safe, fun way to find Internet sites related to this book. All of the sites on FactHound have been researched by our staff.

Here's all you do:

Visit www.facthound.com

Type in this code: 9781404883161

Super-cool stuff! Check out projects, games and lots more at www.capstonekids.com

Thanks to our advisers for their expertise, research, and advice:

Christopher Ruhland, PhD
Professor of Biological Sciences
Department of Biology
Minnesota State University, Mankato

Terry Flaherty, PhD, Professor of English
Minnesota State University, Mankato

Editor: Shelly Lyons
Designer: Alison Thiele
Art Director: Nathan Gassman
Production Specialist: Jennifer Walker
The illustrations in this book were created digitally.

Picture Window Books are published by Capstone,
1710 Roe Crest Drive, North Mankato, Minnesota 56003
www.capstonepub.com

Library of Congress Cataloging-in-Publication Data
Dybvik, Tina.
Sadie's seed adventures : learning about seeds /
by Tina Dybvik ; illustrated by Adam Record.
pages cm. — (Take it outside)
Audience: 4-8.
Audience: K to grade 3
Includes index.
ISBN 978-1-4048-8316-1 (library binding)
ISBN 978-1-4795-1937-8 (paperback)
ISBN 978-1-4795-1902-6 (ebook pdf)
1. Gardening—Juvenile literature. 2. Seeds—Juvenile
literature. I. Record, Adam, illustrator. II. Title.
SB457.D93 2014
635—dc23   2013006274

Printed in the United States of America in
Stevens Point, Wisconsin.
032013   007227WZF13

LOOK FOR ALL THE BOOKS IN THE TAKE IT OUTSIDE SERIES:

KIT AND MATEO JOURNEY INTO THE CLOUDS — LEARNING ABOUT CLOUDS

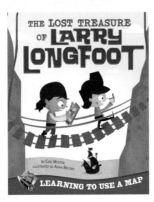

THE LOST TREASURE OF LARRY LONGFOOT — LEARNING TO USE A MAP

SADIE'S SEED ADVENTURES — LEARNING ABOUT SEEDS

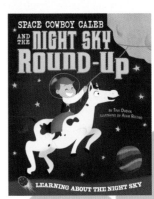

SPACE COWBOY CALEB AND THE NIGHT SKY ROUND-UP — LEARNING ABOUT THE NIGHT SKY